Overview

I have spent the past 20 years working in educational and non-traditional learning communities. I have lived and traveled within and outside of the United States visiting schools and spending time in unique and different learning communities. I have presented nationally and internationally regarding my research in leadership, public schools, popular culture and youth identity. This book is a collection of my thoughts, ideas, and experiences regarding creating engaging, inviting and affirming learning communities for the 21st century. I present ideas and thoughts regarding the actions of transformational educational leaders, successful school administrators, successful teachers, successful parents, and successful students. I also present ideas and thoughts from those individuals who have experienced success with working with Black and Latino males. I hope you find the pages here informative, accessible and transformational. Be well, Dr. G.

201+ Strategies for Successfully Transforming Today's Schools:

A Resource Guide for Educational Leaders, School Administrators, Teachers, Parents, and Students

C. P. Gause, PhD

TABLE OF CONTENTS

Keys for Successful School Administrators

Creating successful learning communities will require **school administrators** to do the following:

First and foremost successful school administrators along with the members of the learning communities in which they lead must develop a vision of learning that promotes success.

This process takes into account standards driven curricula, federal legislation, and/or policies that speak to educational standards. The very core of this vision is based upon one "key" foundational and cultural leadership principle: **All members of the learning community regardless of backgrounds are provided opportunities for academic success.**

Be able to answer the following questions, "What do we want?" and "How are we going to get there?"

Successful educational leaders know in order to answer those questions they must engage in the following:

- Seek information from all community members
- Be reflective in the data that is gathered
- Knowledgeable regarding how to seek information
- Establishing a plan that is attainable and meaningful to EVERYONE
- Goal oriented but not data driven
- Delegating and executing roles and duties but with AFFIRMATION
- Engaging in Affective and Effective Listening
- Strategize for goal-accomplishment and goal-attainment

- Provide learning community members with RESOURCES
- Realize you can not please everyone; however, you can RESPECT everyone

Build open and trusting relationships with your students, faculty, staff, and parent community. This is the key to developing a successful school.

Sustainable change, in a learning community, occurs when trusting relationships have been developed. People are willing to try new and innovating ideas when support from colleagues and supervisors is evident. This support comes in multiple forms and successful administrators understand how to tap into specific resources to provide the right type of support for all members of the community, individually and collectively.

Transform ordinary schools into vibrant learning communities that are creative, equitable, and "just."

Creative learning communities ignore rules; they seek to develop procedures for encouraging desirable behavior versus establishing levels of discipline and punishment. These communities also look for innovations in providing optimal learning experiences for their stakeholders. Creative learning communities remain on the cutting edge and they do this by establishing new missions, thriving on unpredictability and broadening their scope for new horizons. They avoid the mechanization, simplification, and predictability found in custodial organizations.

Seek multiple methods and techniques to promote a school culture that is positive and inviting.

Culture includes both past and present perceptions; and its perceived reality is reflected in its symbols, rituals, and purpose.

The school's culture is a representation of what its members collectively develop as their vision; it is their self-concept. The school's culture reflects what the stakeholders value and what they express to others as being "important around here." In order for school reform to occur educators must realize that the culture of the school and the way the school operates must be transformed inside and out, not only physically but mentally as well.

Affirm, encourage, and support all members of the learning community.

Teachers are the troops. They must be "handled with care" for the vision and mission of a successful learning community to be realized. It is the job, duty, and responsibility of the school administrator to provide all the necessary resources to insure effective instruction. Without adequate instructional tools, support, and preparation teachers will not be effective in delivering a top-notch curriculum. The little things do matter. *Schools that are successful are lead by transformative leaders.*

Transformative leaders continually seek out opportunities for improvement. These individuals look for solutions to problems and encourage the free exchange of ideas. No one has all of the answers. Problems are part fact and part perspective. When individuals come together to discuss issues it opens the space for a "dialogic encounter." Within the discussion people's perceptions often change and/or become redefined.

Being an exceptional educational leader requires functioning as an effective school motivator, as well as an effective school administrator. This is accomplished by striving to "do things right" and by "doing the right thing."

Organizations are socially constructed realties that exist in the minds of their collective members as well as in the concrete sets of rules and regulations that those members develop. According

3

to those rules and roles, educators are, indeed, accountable for the dissemination of knowledge. They are also accountable for the advancement of the human spirit! It is important to make organizations effective; it is important, as well, to foster humane social conditions. Remember: we need leaders who will respond to knowledge in ways that will benefit not only the organization and its members, but the social order as well.

Create a culture of Equity.

Equity is not treating everyone "fair" or "equal." Thinking in these terms does not take into account the individual needs of community members. Equity or to be equitable means you will provide resources and make decisions based upon what each teacher, parent, student and/or staff member needs at that moment in time. Being equitable does not mean showing favoritism to certain individuals and/or groups of people.

Be Inclusive.

Much of school culture at all levels is designed to exclude and not include. Our meeting times, the separation of disciplines, the segregation of students, and the types of instruction presented. We separate based on gender, age, color, identity, sexual orientation and ability. Discover ways to bring EVERYONE together regardless of background, ability and/or identity.

- Change the lunch schedule and let all students eat together as a community
- Utilize instructional materials that celebrate diversity and globalization
- Establish vertical and horizontal planning teams

- Utilize community-partner resources to provide training in diversity
- Allow technology to open the doors for students to communicate across borders
- Identify difference as a strength and utilize it to empower EVERYONE

Diversity is the key.

Create a Culture of Diversity by celebrating difference. Establish a vision and mission for the 21st century by giving your school community resources for globalization. We have the ability to communicate via the Internet across the globe at a moment's notice. Utilize the World Wide Web and all of the applications available to empower your teachers and students to engage in cross-cultural communication.

Create a Professional Learning Community (PLC)

Professional Learning Communities are those designed and developed to increase student's academic success and academic achievement by focusing on instruction. All members of the learning community should receive training on establishing, maintaining, and sustaining Professional Learning Communities. The Internet is filled with many resources regarding establishing and sustaining Professional Learning Communities, take the time and search the web for PLC resources. To engage in the PLC development process you must do the following:

- Supportive of teachers and their ideas
- Visible and a part of the instructional day
- Lead by example
- Be an Instructional Leader

- Establish honest and "open" communication with EVERYONE
- Allow faculty, staff and students to grow and think critically
- Empower students to make instructional decision
- NOT utilize PLC's to increase test scores
- Be open and responsive to change
- Have a commitment to change and rupture the status-quo

Navigate and Negotiate the Political Climate

School and District-level administrators must realize education is a political experience and paradigm. The selection of teachers, the funding of schools, and the communities in which reside within the school building are all guided by political forces. Successful educational leaders are not only aware of the political structures, they know how to navigate and negotiate the political terrain with ease and success. Successful administrators have the uncanny ability to engage in the "sea of politics" without abandoning the cargo and passengers of their ship.

Empower and Facilitate, but Do Not Judge.

Successful educational leaders facilitate the leadership and instructional process for members of the learning community. They do not judge, nor condemn. They inspire and transform the community by doing the following:

- Provide a culture and climate where continuously learning takes place
- Facilitates the learning process
- Create relationships and respect

- Lead with understanding and compassion
- Not be a YES-person, but facilitates the development of SOUND decisions
- Know the various cultures and sub-cultures within the school community
- Know the students, parents and teachers and other community members very well
- Understand their job requires them to be available 24-hours of the day
- Identify pockets of resistance and utilize them as metric for success

A Quick Message for Administrators

Whether you are a College President, Superintendent, Building Principal, Vice-Principal, District-level administrator, or the Director of Special Programs, successful educational leaders and/or school administrators understand the importance of developing engaging, dynamic, and affirming learning communities which provide successful educational experiences for all community members. These individuals seek to transform the lives of individuals in order to be a better future and brighter tomorrow. They realize their success is not measured by what they receive, but by what they give DAILY to those who depend on them. These individuals also realize it is a path less traveled and often times one that endures great pain, heartache, and suffering. Successful educational leaders also realize this path is one filled with great joy, job satisfaction, and triumph. Successful administrators know the knowledge, gifts, and tools they possess serve as a means of facilitating successful learning experiences for young people on a daily basis. They desire that those in which they lead and serve have the opportunity to become great in their chosen professions.

Keys for Successful Teachers

Creating successful learning communities will require **teachers** to do the following:

Job satisfaction is based upon what you give and not what you get; pour your heart and soul into your students so they will become agents of change and democracy.

The new millennium has arrived and schools are still faced with issues of power, race, identity, violence, and ethics, because of this the meaning and purpose of schooling is being redefined. Do you teach for freedom and democracy or to develop a citizenry that will maintain the "status quo?"

Successful teachers have the following qualities:

- Trustworthy
- Loyal
- Goal oriented
- Motivated
- Dedicated
- Persistent
- Open-minded
- Reflective
- Believe in Inquiry
- Excellent conversation skills: listening, questioning, responding
- Believe in themselves
- Believe in Equity, Social Justice, Diversity and Inclusion
- Committed to increasing student achievement and student success

Spend more time looking for solutions than discussing the problems.

The amount of time wasted talking about the problem triples, yielding; time wasted. The amount of time spent on developing a solution increases exponentially when the solution is implemented, yielding time saved and time gained.

Conduct weekly conferences with your students and make a point to address their concerns before you discuss yours.

Begin the conference by asking student if they have questions and/or concerns. Listen to your students attentively without interrupting and allow them to present all of their concerns without value judging them. Use this time to teach them how to engage in a dialogue.

Successful teachers do the following:

- Build trust with their students, parents and other community members
- Give critical time and care to decision making
- Believe in themselves
- Are very perceptive, intuitive and cognizant of others' thoughts and feelings
- Committed to their students and learning community
- Believe in creating positive change
- Collaborate with others
- Seek knowledge, but realize they do not know EVERYTHING
- Believe in providing successful learning experiences for all students
- Create centers for inquiry

- Engage students in thinking critically about the world in which they inhabit
- Provide resources for students to engage themselves and others
- Realize the importance of group learning and professional development

Making a difference in the lives of young people requires every fiber in the fabric of your "being."

Teaching in the 21st century is hard work. The competing forces of Popular Culture and individualism often times present great challenges in order to overcome those challenges you must establish genuine lines of communication with your students. Establish rapport, relationships and realness this will give you more credibility then knowing your discipline.

Be the #1 advocate for your students and they in turn will become your #1 supporter.

Just because the relationship between you and your students may enter a difficult and critical stage still seek to create a space within the learning community to allow the democratic process to take place. In the process do not give up on them and they will not give up on you. Allow your students to voice their concerns and utilize this time to teach them how to do this with civility. Build their character and affirm their spirits.

Teaching is an investment in the future.

We live in a culture that dictates you should witness immediate returns on your investment. Forget about the immediate return. You only see the growth in your investment as it matures. Apply this principle to the students in whom you serve. They come to you at one level of maturity and as you invest in them they grow. The more you invest the bigger your return.

Students believe the knowledge they have is of greater value.

Allow students to engage in the democratic process by usurping authority, bolstering their own position, and discounting your knowledge and wisdom. Teach them how to do this with dignity and respect. The ability to communicate and articulate their position in a manner that is conducive to the learning environment will foster an understanding of peace and justice.

Give of yourself, time, knowledge, and skills to serve humanity.

Remember when you decided to become a member of the teaching profession. By making that decision you decided to give of yourself in all aspects of your life to serve humanity. Yes, what great responsibility and challenge. Are you still up for the task?

Realize you are teaching the "Echo-boomers" and develop strategies to educate them on the importance of earning their way through life.

An echo is given a free space to roam without parameters, guidance, or structure. It continues on its journey until it strikes an object or barrier; then it returns to its point of origination. This generation is the "echo" generation. They have been given everything and when they hit a barrier they return for more things. Instead of things teach them the ability to think "critically."

Utilize your students' daily life experiences to make connections to the lessons you are teaching.

Youth are experiencing a world very differently than they way many of us experienced it during our childhood, adolescence, and/or young adult years. I still remember 45 records, albums and graphic album covers, the music of the 70's, 80's, and early 90's as entered young adulthood. Computers were still relatively new and very expensive and cellular phones came with a bag. There was no globalization and no Smart phones. The world is different now. Utilize your students lived experiences to make their knowledge production and acquisition more exciting and engaging.

Allow students to utilize their technology to teach you something new.

We spend too much time in schools policing students and their technology. Teach them how to utilize technology responsibly. Also, allow students to utilize their technology to teach you something new. These tools can be utilized as instructional devices. They should not be seen as barriers to learning.

Listen to popular music at least once a week to share a common experience with your students outside of the classroom.

Popular music has always had an impact upon the lives of young people. Throughout history parents and teachers alike have strived to teach young people to arm and protect themselves from the ideological power of popular music. Utilize your listening experience to establish a "point of entry" for conversations with your students. With YouTube, iPods, iTunes and the availability of music at our figure tips via the computer, utilize the multiple genres available to teach Language Arts, mathematics, and science. Be hip and cool in your instructional delivery, this will bring your lessons to life.

Seize every opportunity to create a "space for change. You are the Facilitator of the learning process and learning is about change! Remember:

- Change is a process

- Change is accomplished through individuals
- Change is a highly personalized process
- Change involves developmental growth
- Change is socially constructed and context specific

Believe in the work that you do and know that you make a difference in the lives of young people daily.

As educators it is your responsibility and duty to liberate, educate, and motivate individuals towards social transformation. Without you the ideas of democracy and social justice are just that—ideas. Students depend on your nurturing and guidance to enter, explore, and engage the world around them. Be the light for so many who are on the educational path of discovery. Do the following:

- Model the scientific method and read aloud to students
- Let students move around the classroom and drive the curriculum
- Build centers for all students regardless of the age and/or subject
- Conduct experiments inside and outside of the classroom
- Utilize technology daily and in as many lessons as possible
- Collaborate with your students on their learning goals
- Teach everyday like it is your LAST DAY ON EARTH!!!

Say what you mean and mean what you say.

Language, verbal and nonverbal, is the method in which humans develop understanding. The messages we send should be clear and concise. All educational jargon should be eliminated when we speak to members of our community. Much of what we say is often misinterpreted and/or reinterpreted with a new and different meaning. The elimination of education jargon will bring everyone close to achieving the same goals and objectives.

A menial struggle yields menial results; however, a great struggle yields great results.

The struggle in delivering successful academic programs involves negotiating two sets of goals. First, students and their development should be the primary focus of schools. Secondly, the schooling process should be designed to deliver instruction and knowledge to prepare a citizenry who will perpetuate notions of democracy. Together we must face the struggle of educating our citizenry with nobility and commitment. For together in the struggle we are one.

Utilize multiple learning modalities to tap into the individual learning strengths of your student

Students learn differently. They receive, process, analyze and report information in multiple ways. Our Sensory Receptors-- taste, touch, sight, smell, feel, and hearing operate differently individually and collectively as human beings. There is no right way or wrong way for human beings to access information utilizing their senses. Kids access information in their environment utilizing several of them at a time. One sense may be dominant than the other while gathering information. The brain is stimulated and acquires information through our sense. So teachers should provide instructional materials in the following modalities:

- Kinesthetic-Allow kids to move while you are teaching
- Tactile-Allow kids to touch and manipulate objects while you are teaching

- Auditory-Allow kids to listen to different objects related to your lesson while you are teaching
- Visual-Allow kids to see multiple objects using various media while you are teaching
- Olfactory-Allow kids to smell different objects related to your lesson while you are teaching

Promote creativity in a non-hostile learning environment.

Successful teachers of successful learning communities know the importance of providing students with the opportunity to take risks in engaging the learning environment, but with affirmation, care and great facilitation. These teachers provide the following environment and/or do the following things:

- Speak with a warm and affirming, but firm voice
- Do not yell in learning environment unless everyone is cheering for a team
- Respect EVERYONE and operate out of an "ethic of care"
- Create a healthy atmosphere of COLLABORATION
- Create a LEARNING LAB CULTURE within the learning community
- PRAISE students!
- Establish friendly non-punitive routines
- Establish classroom POLICIES, PROCEDURES and CONSEQUENCES
- Allow student to work in cooperative groups for 60% of instructional time
- MOTIVATE

- Realize young people are not adults and then ..e atmosphere within the learning community to celebrate youth culture
- Create a learning community climate where MISTAKES ARE CELEBRATED
- Extend the learning community outside of the school building by taking students on field-experiences
- View the school as living systems and maintaining and sustaining a healthy vibrant LIFE is the most important function of the educational process
- Include PARENTS in all aspects of the learning community

A Quick Message for Teachers

Teaching is by far one of the most difficult professions. We are called upon to solve all of societal ills through the educational process, as well as teach children who come from very difficult backgrounds. I still believe teaching is the noblest of all professions and often remind many of my students, educators, friends, and colleagues that without teachers no other profession on earth would exist. Given all of the budgetary cuts because of the recent economic crisis in our nation, for the first time in a generation teachers have been eliminated nationally across the United States. The most important profession did not go untouch during the very difficult times of 2007, 2008, and 2009. Because many teachers left the profession, those who remain are feeling the weight and burden of a system in distress. You have more students to teach and fewer resources to teach them. You made have experienced a cut in your paycheck and you realize now more than ever schools are viewed as the answer for society's problems. You are also witnessing the lives of Middle Class America disappear and the number of children and families in poverty increase exponentially. The amount of paperwork is insurmountable, the number of students who are identified as English Language Learners (ELL) and/or those with Limited English Proficiency (LEP) increase exponentially. They are appearing in your classrooms with no support and the teaching assistant you had last year now works in the cafeteria if she works at all. Yes, our profession is in crisis and there appears to be new end in sight. You are being forced to "teach to the test." You don't like this idea, but the new pay scale adopted by your district ties your pay to student growth. What are you going to do? You are tired, worn out and disgusted. There is no "work-life" balance and you are also trying to maintain a household filled with its own troubles. I want you to know, I other thousands like me support

21

you. The students who sit in your classroom day in and day out need you. Parents as difficult as some of them are would not know what to do if you were not there. You are THE ROCK! What you do is vital to the continuation of our humanity. Don't give up as hard as it seems, because a child depends on your instruction, your encouragement, your attention. I do I know this, because I was once that child! If my teachers had given up on me and/or the system, you would not be reading this book. I thank you for all you do in the name of education. I appreciate the knowledge, skills, gifts and talents you bring daily to the classroom. Our entire society, nation and world are indebted to you! Without you, where would we be? THANK YOU FOR TEACHING ME! Thank you for continuing to meet the daily challenges of the profession. I SALUTE YOU for your efforts.

Instructional Best Practices for Teachers

Strategies and Techniques for Teaching Reading (Literature)

Teachers should do more of the following:

Read aloud to students daily

Schedule time for independent and group reading

Encourage students to choose their own reading materials

Expose students to multiple types of genres of literature

Encourage students to read fiction, non-fiction, science fiction and mystery books

Model and discuss your own reading practices

Place emphasis on comprehension, context and genre

Teach reading as a process:

- Use strategies that activate prior knowledge
- Help students make and test predictions
- Structure help during reading
- Provide after-reading applications

Encourage social and collaborative activities with much discussion and group by interest and book choice

Silent reading should be followed by in-depth discussions

Teach literacy skills within the context of whole and meaningful literature

The Writing Process and Writing activities should occur before and after reading activities

Use content specific text by discipline (e.g., historical novels in social studies)

Evaluate student progress by focusing on higher-order thinking skills

Teachers should do less of the following:

Emphasize whole-class reading-group activities

Selecting all reading materials for individual/groups

Rely on basal readers

Keeping own reading habits private

Emphasizing reading sub-skills (word analysis, syllabication and phonics)

Teach the reading process as a single, one-step act

Individual seat/desk work

Establish reading groups by reading ability/level

Round-robin oral reading

Teaching skills in phonics workbooks/drills in isolation

Limiting time to engage in the writing process

Discouraging pre-conventional spelling

Maintaining an established reading time

Focusing on individual low-level sub-skills

Measuring student reading success by a test score

Strategies for Teaching Writing

Teachers should do more of the following:

Student responsibility and ownership:

- Allow students to choose their topics and measures for improvement
- Conduct brief teacher-student conferences
- Teach students how to review and monitor their progress

Class time spent on developing original work through:

- Establish real purposes for writing based on students' lived experiences
- Encourage students' to become involved in the writing process
- Provide instruction for all stages of the writing process
- Utilize the Prewriting, drafting, revising, editing cycle

Model for students—drafting, revising, editing and sharing—as fellow author

Teach grammar and mechanics in context, specifically at the editing stage, and as needed

Teach students that Writing is for real audiences and personal pleasure

Publish works for the class, school and greater community

27

Establish an affirming and supportive classroom setting for shared learning:

- Actively exchange students' ideas
- Value students' language and work
- Promote small and large-group collaboration
- Establish and encourage the peer critiquing and review process for improvement

Utilize writing across the curriculum as a tool for learning

Constructive and efficient evaluation that involves:

- Provide informal and brief responses while students work
- Evaluate and assessment a few student generated polished pieces
- Focus only on a few errors at a time
- Look for overall growth in students' self-evaluation
- Encourage open honest expression and risk taking

Teachers should do less of the following:

Controlling decision making by:
- Deciding all writing topics
- Dictating suggestions for improvement
- Determining all learning objectives
- Delivering whole-group instruction only

Significant amount of instructional time spent on isolated drills on "sub-skills" (grammar, vocabulary, spelling, paragraphing, penmanship etc.)

Briefly giving writing assignments without context or purpose, all in one step

Talking about the writing process, but models or shares

Delivering isolated grammar lessons in order based on textbook

Teacher is the only one who reads assignments and/or student work

Devaluation of students' ideas by:

- Viewing students as individuals with limited knowledge and language abilities
- Treats students as a group of competing individuals
- Focusing too much on students who are viewed as cheating, disruptive

Writing taught only during "language arts" period, infrequently, and/or not at all.

Evaluation as negative burden for teacher and student by:

- Grading papers heavily for errors only
- Editing papers instead of allowing the student make improvements
- Grading is punitive, primary focus on errors and not growth

Strategies for Teaching Mathematics

Teachers should do more of the following:

Connect mathematics instruction to real-life "lived-experiences"

Use manipulative as much as possible

Encourage students to engage in cooperative/collaborative groups

Discuss mathematics and bring in real life applications, daily

Encourage students to engage in questioning

Teach students how to provide rationales and justifications for answers

Write about mathematics

Instruction should focus on Problem-solving

Content integration is key

Use computers, graphing calculators and iPhone applications

Facilitate the learning process

Evaluate and assess learning as an integral part of instruction

Teach mathematics as a major tool of real-life problem solving

Provide multiple Word problems with a variety of structures and solutions

Engage students in everyday real world problems and applications

Incorporate multiple Problem-solving strategies in lessons

Provided open-ended problems

Provided extended problem-solving projects as a form of instruction

Formulate and investigate questions from real-life problem situations

Teach mathematics as a form of communication and language

Discuss Mathematics

Read Mathematics

Engage students in lessons on inductive and deductive reasoning

Teachers should do less of the following:

Utilizing the mathematics textbook at the expense of real-life problem-solving

Lessons which engage rote practice

Lessons requiring students to engage in Rote memorization of rules and formulas

Encourage students to seek single answers and single methods to find answers

A significant amount of instructional time and learning activities dedicated to the use of drill worksheets

A significant amount of time dedicated to repetitive written exercises and practice

Teaching by telling and not by modeling

Teaching computation out of context

Overly stressing Memorization

Giving students mathematics tests for grades only and not to see students' growth

Establishing and maintaining a classroom where the teacher is viewed as the dispenser of knowledge

Discounting the importance of mathematics integration with other subjects and/or disciplines

Utilizing cue words for operation exercises

Significant practice on routine and one-step problems

Significant practice on problems by type

Communicating verbally and non-verbally mathematics as a difficult subject and only few students will ever master the subject

Relying heavily on fill-in-the-blank worksheets

Allowing students to answer problems with yes or no responses

Allowing students to answer questions that need only numerical responses

Encouraging students to identify complex problems in simple terms

Relying on the teacher and/or answer key

Strategies for Teaching Science

Teachers should do more of the following:

Hands-on activities that include:

- Students identifying their own questions the natural world
- Observation learning activities designed by students
- Instructional activities which focus on discovery and inquiry
- Students encouraged to hypothesize to explain data
- Instruction that allows students to engage the investigation process prior to information being presented
- Students engage in self reflection throughout the instructional learning and activity process to realize concepts learned
- Instructional activities which provide application to social issues, environmental concerns and/or further scientific inquiry

Large and small group instruction should focus on underlying concepts about our natural world and how phenomena are explained.

Questioning, thinking, and problem solving, especially:

- Encourage students to question common and/or long held beliefs
- Establish a willingness to embrace ambiguity when data aren't decisive
- Create a classroom/laboratory environment which encourages students to be open to changing their opinion

- Use logic, plan inquiry-based activities, hypothesizing, inferring

Utilize technology in instructional delivery and activities as much as possible

Facilitate in-depth study of important thematic topics

Create a classroom culture of curiosity regarding nature and positive attitudes toward science for all students, including females and members of minority groups

Integrate reading, writing, and math in science instruction and units

Establish collaborative small working groups with a focus on learning for all group members

Evaluation and assessment should focus on scientific concepts, processes, and attitudes

Teachers should do less of the following:

Delivering science instruction based mainly on lecture and information giving

Depending on textbooks and simplistic patterns of instruction

Lab experiences where students follow steps without their own question

Treating students as if they have no knowledge or investigative abilities

Rote memorization of vocabulary, definitions, and explanations without connection to broader ideas

Encouraging students to work independently and competitively

Correcting students' perceptions of direct instruction

Isolating science from students' everyday lives and lived experiences

Superficial coverage of material based on scope-and-sequence

Believing only a few brilliant "nerds" can enjoy or succeed in science study

Instructional activities limited to texts, lectures, and multiple-choice quizzes

Teacher viewed as expert in subject matter versus students being seen as experts as well

Evaluation and assessment focusing on memorization of detail and ignoring thinking skills, process skills, and attitudes

Strategies for Teaching Social Studies

Teachers should do more of the following:

Create a classroom that encourages students of all ability levels to engage in interactive and cooperative learning

Provide instructional activities encouraging students to make choices about what to study

Create an environment where students discover the complexities of human interaction

Integrate social studies with other areas of the curriculum (e.g., language arts, science, mathematics)

Provide instruction whereby students engage in inquiry and problem solving related to significant human issues

Create a classroom culture whereby students make decisions and participate in wider social, political, and economic affairs; by doing so will develop a sense of shared responsibility for the welfare of their school and community

Provide richer and deeper levels of content in all grade levels, building on the prior knowledge children bring to social studies topics; this includes study of concepts from psychology, sociology, economics, and political science, as well as history and geography; students of all ages can understand, within their experience, American social institutions, issues for social groups, and problems of everyday living

Provide instruction whereby students value and experience a "sense" of connected with humanity across American and global history, realizing the history and culture of diverse social groups, and the environment are all apart of social and historical systems

Encourage students to engage in inquiry with regard to their own cultural groups and communities to promote a sense of ownership

Evaluation and assessment should involve further learning and the promotion of responsible citizenship and open expression of concepts/ideas

Teachers should do less of the following:

Superficial coverage of curriculum based on scope and sequence, which covers everything but allows no time for a deeper understanding of topics

Rote memorization of isolated facts in textbooks

Instruction that isolates students from the actual exercise of responsible citizenship

Significant emphasis on reading about citizenship or future participation in the larger social and political world

Relying heavily on a lecture-style of instructional delivery

- Instructional activities that include only textbook reading and test taking
- Not valuing student interest in social studies
- Leaving out significant curriculum until secondary grades

Engaging in instructional practices that privilege one dominant cultural heritage and/or viewing other cultural heritage as a deficit

Instructional activities that leaves students disconnected and unexcited about social studies

Evaluation and assessment only at the end of a unit or grading period; assessments that test only factual knowledge or memorization of textbook information

Strategies for Teaching the Related Arts

(Visual Arts, Music, Dance, Physical Education, Theatre, Careers & Technology)

Teacher should do more of the following:

Related Arts instruction should focus on doing, learning, and thinking

Instruction should focus on the process of creation, and not on the product

Instruction should highlight the steps and stages of careful craftsmanship

Focus more on student originality, their choice and responsibility in art making

Related Arts should be viewed as an element of talent development for all students and not a select few who you may perceive as being "talented"

Class instruction should focus on the array of art forms, from Western and non-Western sources, different time periods, cultures, and ethnic groups

Develop and support every student's quest to discover his or her personal media, style, and tastes

The Arts should be a viable part of the school day and curriculum

Integrate of related arts across the curriculum

Provide reasonable class loads and work assignments for related arts-specialist teachers and they should not be viewed as "baby-sitters," or proctors for tests

School and classroom instruction should be facilitated by Artists in schools, both as performers and as partners with art teachers

Establish and maintain long-term partnerships with artists and arts organizations

Every member of the school community and the greater community-at large should be involved with the Arts.

Teacher should do less of the following:

Emphasizing the studying of other people's artworks

Art instruction and/or projects requiring students to create identical products

Extreme focus on final products and not celebrating learning process

Encouraging students to view Art (Related Arts) as an arena for competition, screening, awards, and prizes

Promoting an exclusive focus on Western, high-culture, elite art forms disconnected from a wide range of art making/production

Allowing students to explore too many art forms and not encouraging mastery

Related Arts being relegated only to the Related Arts teachers only and not being provided by the classroom teacher

Arts classes that lack intensity and that occur only once a week.

Overloading related art teachers with multiple classes

Allowing Physical Education to be viewed as only athletics

Utilizing instructional time for skill development and not expression

Believing only certain types of students can participate in the arts program

Stereotyping and/or typecasting students based upon race, class and gender

Evaluation and Assessment of student progress based upon final products and not growth

Keys for Successful Parents

Creating successful communities will require the parents to do the following:

Believe in your educational system.

As taxpayers, you the parent, are responsible for the education of ALL CHILDREN, not just your own. You must believe in the educational process and commit to insuring all members of the learning community are receiving the needed resources to experience educational success. Believe in the teachers, the administrators, the staff members and above all BELIEVE THEY KNOW WHAT IS BEST!

Support your educational system with as many resources as you can.

Because education is the function of the state, your local and state tax dollars provide substantially more than the federal government. It is still not enough. There are many schools that do not have enough resources for all children; therefore you can do the following:

- Start a clothes closet for your school
- Purchase books for classroom libraries
- Establish a charitable foundation for the school and donate money
- Volunteer as much as you can in schools
- Lobbying local and state leaders to provide additional resources
- Utilize the Internet to galvanize support for schools
- GIVE

Support your children by nurturing the gifts and talents they possess.

Your children are your greatest gifts and you should support the gifts and talents in which they possess with all you have at your disposal. DO NOT SPOIL THEM, but invest in their talents, because the investments will yield great rewards.

Listen to every word your child speaks, by doing so you will come to understand how they view the world in which they live.

Many of us grew up in households where children were seen but not heard; however, now our youth self-segregate because of the kingdoms they have built in their bedrooms. We have little time for dialogue these days with so many responsibilities and so many schedules to navigate. STOP! Take moments daily and listen to your youth, they are experiencing so much in their young lives and many of them are having difficulty coping with the stress. Drugs, alcohol, sex, and/or disengaging from families is the new norm. It doe not have to be this way. STOP! Listen to what they are saying and what they are doing you will be AMAZED!

Set a regular scheduled time to engage in a dialogue with your children daily.

Kids need structure in their lives; however, they should have some freedoms to explore the many opportunities they are presented through their schools, families, church, sports and other organizations and institutions. Kids are over-scheduled, families are over-scheduled and it all out of CONTROL! What are you going to do about it? Eliminate some of the activities and build in time to engage your youth, daily. Cut back and (re) deploy a family time that everyone can adhere. It does not have to be everyday; however, it should occur at least twice a week, not including the weekend.

Intelligence along with wisdom will insure the success of your children.

Your child's success will depend on the wisdom you share. Children are sponges and they soak up everything. Model the behaviors you want to see in your child and discuss with them the characteristics to a successful life. Share with them the concept of CHARACTER and the traits needed in this society to be considered as one with GREAT CHARACTER! Let them know the following are important:

- Kindness
- Compassion
- Honesty
- Integrity
- Patience
- Humbleness
- Respect
- Love
- Faith
- Charity
- Hope
- Temperance
- Persistence
- Determination
- Motivation
- Empathy
- Sympathy
- Commitment
- Sharing
- Joy
- Triumph

- Duty
- Patriotism

Children will remember your indifference and your silence.

It is important to be attentive to youth at all times. Everything they experience is important to them. By showing indifference youth will come to believe that they are not important to you. Silence is only golden when someone else is speaking.

Do not give your children everything.

Giving your children everything creates dependence. Dependence is the precursor to victimization. Teach your child to be independent in mind and deed. Also model the importance of understanding the value of money, worth and ability. Teach them the value of money by showing them how to earn it. When you give a child everything it stifles their ability to understand how to earn what they want. Giving children everything also colludes their understanding of how to place value upon the work in which they do.

Regardless of how you look on the outside the inside really does matter.

Parents often do not like to come to school events because they worry about how they look, especially those parents who are considered to be "working class" and/or in poverty. We are taught the importance of communicating, "who you are" can be surmised in how you walk, the integrity of your reputation, the smile on your face and the clothes in which you wear; however many corporate scandals have revealed that if you look like a million dollars you probably stole it from the stockholders. Parents do not allow how you perceive the way you look keep you from taking an active role in your child's school. Show up and get involved!

Attend all PTA meetings, "Open-houses" and schedule conferences.

As a parent, you must be visible within the school community and also at school functions and events. These are opportunities to show you are engaged in the educational process and you are committed to your child. If you cannot attend any of these events, designate a family member to go as your representative.

Read to your child at least "30" minutes a day.

Reading is a life skill every human being needs in order to function in our society. Reading to your child everyday allows them to hear not on language in use, but also it gives them a connection to your voice and personhood. Reading daily to your child provides a calming effect and a self-assurance. Daily reading brings meaning to life and brings ideas, thoughts and concepts alive. It stimulates the brain and develops the brain's language center.

Monitor the amount of time your child spends in front of the television and playing video games.

Television is a passive activity yielding very little brain stimulation. Video games stimulate the brain and senses in multiple ways; however, too much of it can cause physical and neurological problems. Limit the amount of time your child plays video games and watches television. The best way to do this is to watch television with and/or play video games with them for a designated amount of time daily and/or weekly.

Provide a significant amount of Reading Books for your children.

Your home should be filled with various types of reading materials. A home filled with books, magazines, and newspapers provides a richer environment and children who attend schools from those homes are at or above grade level.

Encourage your child to help prepare a meal to evaluate and teach them "standard units of measurement."

Learning measurement in the abstract is difficult for kids. The best way to teach measurement is to experience measuring objects. Cooking is a great way to learn and practice measuring skills. Some teachers in schools utilize fake pizzas to teach measurement, but what a great way to teach measurement by having your child help cook and/or bake a meal from "scratch." This is also a great time for parent-child bonding. Cooking at home is also a healthy way of eating. Many in young people are suffering from Obesity and diseases related to improper nutrition. Cooking at home provides an opportunity for preparing a well-balanced meal and assist in helping everyone to develop healthy eating habits.

Attend your local school board meetings.

In order to understand the entire public schooling process, you have to attend a school board meeting. As a parent and taxpayer you have a "right" to attend those meetings. Many decisions that impact you, your child and the school community are decided at school board meetings. Contact your local school district and secure the meeting dates, times and locations. Some school districts actually meet out in the community in various schools, others meet at the local district office. The meetings are open and if you would like to address your school board, contact the local district office and ask for the procedures to be added to the agenda to address your local school leaders.

Visit your local Public Library every two weeks.

The Public Library is a great location for gaining reading and/or other sources for your audio-visual enjoyment. It also provides the use of free computers and Internet and there is no cost for checking out books. The Public Library also provides free seminars on various topics of interest and serves as a space for communal socialization.

Volunteer a portion of your time every six weeks in a teacher's classroom.

Volunteering in your child's classroom is very important. Contact the school and find out the procedures to become a volunteer and then do so. It is a rewarding feeling and it allows you the opportunity to develop a relationship with your child's teacher and the school community. You can do the following as a volunteer:

- Read to students
- Work with students on various subjects
- Assist the teacher in doing administrative work
- Assist the teacher in developing instructional activities
- Facilitate learning groups and learning centers
- Provide an extra set of eyes and ears
- Provide a 30 minute relief period for the teacher to re-tool
- Mentor a student and/or group of students
- Assist the teacher in delivering instruction
- Assist the teacher in accelerating the learning process for students
- Assist the teacher in helping student reach their potential

Become a member of the School Improvement Team.

This group is a very important group in the school. The School Improvement Team is comprised of teachers, parents, school administrators, community partners and students. This group is designed to help the school develop a plan to improve the academic success of students and to identify and secure resources to assist teachers in providing optimal learning experiences for their students. The School Improvement Team focuses on helping a school in being successful academically and socially.

Become a member of the Monday Moms volunteer organization at your child's school. If one does not exist create one.

Monday Moms are a very important volunteer group. They work with everyone in the learning community to make the school better for EVERYONE!

Become a member of the Friday Fathers volunteer organization at your child's school. If one does not exist create one.

Friday Fathers are an extremely important volunteer group. Many students have absent fathers at home. This group and **Monday Moms** can do the following:

- Mentor kids
- Supervise playground activities
- Tutor students in various subjects
- Assist the teacher in delivering instruction
- Monitor the halls
- Provide a level of security
- Supervise Field Experiences
- Provide a 30 minute time for the teacher to re-tool

- Allow kids to see them as an integral part of the educational process

Spend time in the Commons Area to observe the activity of the school. By doing so, you will develop an appreciation for the work educators do on behalf of society.

Where kids hangout during their free time during the school day is important; however, what is most important is what they are doing during this free time! Spend time with kids in the Commons Area and/or wherever they are during their free time because you will get an inside look into the activities of their world. It is also a good practice if you are establishing and/or maintaining relationships with your own children. Dropping by the Commons Area will allow you to see the impact of peer pressure on your child as well as all of the other students. It also will help you understand the influence of POPULAR CULTURE!

A Quick Message for Parents

There has never been a time in our history the greatest need for engaging and supportive parents within our schools and learning communities. The economic crisis created a great need for resources in public schools. Many students are experiencing family crises and I realize many of you are the parents of those students. Many of you have lost your jobs, your savings and even your will to keep the family afloat. Your homes have been foreclosed and those of you who have had this experience are now living with relatives, living in shelters, and/or homeless. Those of you who have been fortunate to weather the greatest economic storm of our time are helping needy relatives and families. I salute the work you are doing for our communities. I ask that you remember the children in our schools and continue to seek out opportunities to provide additional resources. Remember the teachers, administrators, staff members, cafeteria staff, bus drivers, custodians, crossing guards, assistants, and volunteers who work with your children every day and who believe in them. Be kind to them because indeed they are feeling your pain, the pain of their students and the pain of the community. Volunteer when you can and encourage others to do so as well. It will take all of us working collaboratively to survive these very arduous and difficult times.

Keys for Successful Students

Creating successful learning experiences will require **students** to do the following:

Be prepared to achieve the impossible regardless of conditions and/or circumstances.

These are tough times for you as a student and as a youth. You have never seen an economic crisis of this nature nor did you ever think one could exist. You never thought there would be so many wars across the globe. You never thought you would have to leave your house, live with neighbors, live with other family members and/or strangers. You had some perspective of safety and a few things provided for you. These are tough times, but you will get through them. You must do your best and strive for excellence in all that you do.

Integrity is your moral compass.

If you are going to be a part of the crowd, be the leader and lead with integrity. Earn your way through school by doing your best with all of the power that lies within you. Complete all assignments on time and with integrity. Do not settle for mediocrity and understand that your participation in the educational process is not a sport or extra-curricular activity, it is your job!

You exist in body, mind and spirit; therefore, cultivate and nurture every aspect of your being.

To achieve greatness you must cultivate and nurture every part of your being. In order to be successful you must do the following:

- Exercise your body daily
- Exercise your mind daily
- Practice your faith daily
- Eat a well balance meal
- Read daily
- Study daily
- Develop a plan with goals and objectives
- Execute your plan
- Monitor and adjust your plan for success
- Listen intently to your elders for wisdom and for instruction from adults

Envision where you want to go and what you want to achieve in life and then focus all of your energy towards the outcomes.

Whatever goal and/or life plan you have for yourself you must focus all of your energies on completing this plan. In order for this plan to come to pass it must be a plan of good and not evil and one that is not selfish or self-centered. It should be a plan designed to provide enough resources for a great life; however, it should not take advantage others nor allow for you to attain your goal at the expense of others.

Honesty, integrity, truth, justice and respect coupled with hard work, dedication, compassion, and love will determine your success, not the amount of money you earn.

Money has nothing to do with success. Success is measured by how much you give to others and the impact you have on the communities in which you inhabit. Success is about making the world a better place for EVERYONE!

Nothing in life is fair; however, you have the power to make it "just."

Life is not fair! It will never be fair! There will be pain, heartache and challenges; however; you have the power to make life JUST! Decide on treating everyone with care and respect, regardless of how they treat you and seek to be "just" in the decisions you make so that everyone benefits and no one walks away feeling like a loser.

A change in your behavior is the only thing that will change your outcome.

If you want to see a change in the outcomes and events in your life, you must change your behavior. It takes 30 days to develop a healthy habit, but nearly a lifetime to break a bad one. Develop healthy habits of mind and heart and exercise them daily.

Commitment to your dreams and goals will get you closer to achieving them then your talent alone.

Goal attainment is more about commitment than talent. Talent is only a small part of the equation. This is the equation for success $2C + T = S$. It takes double the Commitment plus Talent to achieve Success. You must stick to what you believe and work hard at realizing your dreams. It can be done but not without great cost and sacrifice.

Transform your community by engaging in volunteerism and community service.

Everything we have in our society came with the price of Blood, Sweat, and Tears. Volunteering and engaging in community service is your return on the investment many have made in you and your success. You owe your community and those who are a part of it for the opportunity to live, to work and to pursue your education. GIVE BACK! It's not only the right thing to do; it is your responsibility as a citizen of this humanity.

Let go of old hurt, pain and regret they only serve as stumbling blocks towards achieving your destiny.

Forgive those who wrong you and ask forgiveness from those you have wronged. Life is a precious gift and the loss of life can be traumatic. It is better to live in peace and harmony then in regret.

Conflict is a natural occurring phenomenon, how you deal with conflict will be the anomaly.

There will be conflict in your life. This is a part of the Circle of Life. How you deal with conflict will determine your character. Be kind, but firm; caring, but strong; and affirming; but resilient. These are the tests of your character. Do not bully, become hostile, seek to sabotage or assassinate someone's character.

Listen before speaking, and then decide if what you have to say is important enough to share with everyone.

We live in a time where everyone is talking to someone. We are doing a lot of talking but very little listening. We should reduce the amount of time we talk by doubling the amount of time we listen. Listen to not just speech, but to the environment. Many of life's lessons can be heard in nature.

Treat your siblings with love and respect, because one day they may be your employer.

Brothers and sisters, your siblings; may often get on your nerves. You may have a bad relationship with one or more of them; however, be kind because one day they could be your employer. I know this can be difficult, but take time to get to know your siblings as individuals so when you become adults' fond memories of your childhood will exist. Respect your siblings like adults and don't live in the past by reminding them of stuff that happened in childhood.

Limit the amount of time you spend in the virtual world on social networking sites.

Spend less time in the virtual world and more time in physical contact with people. The spirit of our humanity is only synergistic when human beings are in physical contact with one another. Technology has become a tool that maintains separation. It should be tool to bring us together virtually and physically.

Volunteer your time and a portion of your earnings once a month to a charity that aid the needy.

Giving to charity is an important part of our humanity. It teaches us how to share our resources and it provides opportunities for expressing gratefulness and gratitude. Through your synagogue, temple, church and/or local agency give back to your community. Serving those in your community is indeed noble. Serving humanity is indeed greatness.

You are closer to greatness than you think.

Do not quit when times are the most difficult, because greatness is close by. If you truly believe you have given it all you got and you have done your best then complete that path with dignity and respect and move on to the next path.

Your knowledge, skills, and dispositions (attitudes) serve as the foundation to your academic success.

School is a place for inquiry, knowledge production and knowledge attainment. As you learn new skills they build upon others previously learned. The process of acquiring knowledge and producing knowledge is two sides of the same coin. Your attitude while gaining and sharing knowledge serves as the gatekeeper to gaining more and sharing more. If you want to success academically then sharpen your skills, gain more knowledge and have a great attitude in the process.

Perseverance is the key to overcoming all of life's challenges.

The only way to overcome the pain, heartache and challenges of life you must persevere. Life will continue to present opportunities and challenges for victory or defeat. It is up to you how you will engage. Don't give up nor give in if you want to experience success and build your character. You must keep fighting. Those who stay in the fight will ultimately win. You must challenge yourself to gain greater strength for the fight before you. Endure life's challenges and you will be rewarded.

Honor your parents, your teachers, your friends, your neighbors, and yourself.

There is no cost to HONOR someone. Be good to those around you and in your communities and by doing so you bring great HONOR to yourself.

Just because you can does not mean you always should.

Do not do something just because you can. Many are imprisoned, incapacitated and entombed because they did something just because they could. It is better to be cautious and advantageous than to be foolish and reckless. Opportunities will always come your way; however, it is important to choose wisely and carefully those in which you will engage.

Acknowledge your God-given gifts, talents, and knowledge by utilizing them for good and not evil.

Seek to do what is right at all times and forsake all that is evil. Your knowledge, gifts, and talents were granted to you to transform your community and to be independent. They are not designed for the trappings of selfishness. The talents, gifts, and knowledge placed within you by the "Divine Creator" should be utilized for the good of the community and not selfish gain.

Determine to be the best and the brightest in all aspects of your life and share that belief with everyone.

By challenging and loving yourself for who you are is the first key to being the best and brightest. What you do for those that are around you will speak to the fulfillment of your life. Developing and maintaining a positive attitude is the second key to being the best and brightest. By doing so you realize failure is not an option and does not exist when you exercise your beliefs.

Dress for Success

Getting ahead in life requires a certain style of dress. You must dress for success and not based upon the elements of Popular Culture and fashion. Many of the outfits and styles you see are not designed for the workplace. If you load your closet up with the latest styles and fashions and do not have the proper attire for a job interview you have just eliminated 80% of your success. Look your best, feel your best and be your best.

A Quick Message to Students

You who enter and walk the halls of today's public schools are younger than MTV, have witnessed the birth and rise of Google, Yahoo, the iPod and the iPhone. You were born after the fall-out of the first Gulf War, and witnessed the beginning of the second Gulf War. You have witnessed your friends, family members and loved ones go to the Iraq Ware and War in Afghanistan. Many of you believe casting a vote for the next American Idol is a proper form of exercising democracy and your right to vote. You have witnessed the shift from the War on Drugs to the War on Terrorism. Many of you witnessed the possible impeachment of a sitting President, the fall of Enron, General Motors, Chrysler, Lehman Brothers, AIG and the greatest economic downturn since The Great Depression of the 1920's and 1930's. Many of you are witness the great disparity between the wealth and the poor. You are receiving your formal K-12 education in re-segregated public schools, 50+ years after the landmark decision of Brown v. Board of Education of Topeka 1954 by the United States Supreme Court ending public school segregation. You have lived through the attack on the World Trade Center and two of the most horrific natural disasters of human record, The Tsunami of Indonesia and Hurricane Katrina of the United States. You have witnessed the failure of the United States government to protect basic human rights, but yet the election of the first African American President of the United States, Barack H. Obama.

Your lives today are filled with Blogs, MySpace, Facebook, Chatrooms, Instant Messaging, Cellular phones with individualized ringtones and the ability to go Wi-Fi through virtual portals and entry points located in various locales across America. The Internet has become the vehicle for global socialization and information. Media outlets constantly bombard you with situations and circumstances that are detrimental to the human condition such as war, famine, disease and greed. It occurs so frequently I am concerned for your emotional, mental and physical health. I believe you have become anesthetized to it. You are experiencing substance abuse at alarming rates, particularly as it relates to prescription drugs. You are participating in the "underworld" economy at epidemic proportions while falling behind your global peers in math and science. You are inadequately prepared by public schools to continue your pathway towards higher education and once you get to college you are unable to afford the tuition to remain. All is not lost. I have faith and hope in you. Your generation is the generation that will lead America into greatness. You will set the new environmentally friendly policies. It is you who will demand and realize International Human Rights. It is you who will insure everyone has Universal Healthcare and a Living Wage. I have hope in you, but you must keep the faith, fight the good fight and persevere! YOU ARE OUR ONLY HOPE! OUR HOPE LIES IN YOU!

Keys For Working Successfully With Black/Latino Males

Creating successful learning communities requires ALL of us to help our brothers to realize their dreams and goals. Black and Latino males as a demographic in proportion to the United States population has the highest, drop-out rate, incarceration rate, and mortality rate. In order to change this successful educational leaders, parents, community leaders, advocates, university-partnerships, school administrators, teachers, superintendents, district-level administrators, clergy, policy-makers, politicians, activists and people must do the following:

Speak truth to power.

Tell the truth and hold our brothers to a higher standard than they have for themselves and by doing the following:

- We must engage in a dialogue with them to understand their needs and then provide support mechanisms to insure those needs are met.
- We must establish and maintain high expectations regardless of situation and circumstance.
- We must forgive them for their wrongs.
- Love them unconditionally and not put up with any of their failures or excuses.
-

Engage in intellectual enterprise.

Providing opportunities for knowledge production and knowledge acquisition is key to successfully working with Male Students of Color. They must receive a formal education and given mentorship to successfully navigate and negotiate the educative process.

Engage in a work ethic based on integrity.

We must mentor our brothers into a work ethic of integrity. We must encourage them to being committed to their own self-development. We must convince them to delay immediate gratification and invest in lifelong learning with the understanding they will see the fruits of their labor sooner than they think. We must also establish community-based employer-partnerships. Many of these young men have experienced the juvenile justice system and will need programs to help them develop a work ethic that is based upon trust, honesty and mutual respect. It will take preparation, patience, and perseverance.

Engage in spiritual practice and a renewing of your faith daily.

Working with these young men will require you to establish a relationship based upon faith. Black and Latino males come from families with strong faith traditions. Practicing your faith maybe the catalyst to assisting them in establishing or reconnecting with their own faith practices.

Empower and Embrace the multiple identities they perform.

Males of Color like to "posture" and express themselves in a myriad of ways. Their expressions the multiple identities they perform should be viewed as strength and should be utilized in the educational process. These young men are communal in nature and enjoy being a part of a collective. Respect their feelings, thoughts, and ideologies and remember to maintain high expectations, you will have to express this to them constantly. Why? Because for many of them they have been told they are failures and for most of them they have not experienced any level of success. The following can be done to provide stability:

- Do not be dismissive about who they believe themselves to be
- Maintain high expectations and often express them consistently
- Provide ongoing timelines for tasks to be completed, particularly in relation to classroom instruction
- Seek to be "just," not fair
- Be equitable in your decisions about consequences and enforcing policies.

Build unguarded bridges across the multiple landscapes we inhabit so that Black and Latino males will feel open to crossing those bridges without fear and retribution.

By deconstructing your biases and by binge open and honest about your own perspective you develop an unguarded bridge for Males of Color to cross and explore. This is the prerequisite to building authentic relationships and for maintaining open communication. If you do not know the answer to a question, be honest in communicating this and seek their input. Encourage a relationship whereby they will trust you to ask them to join you in discovering the answers to school and life.

Mentor Black and Latino males beyond the occasional lunches and social outings to engage them intellectually, socially, spiritually, and emotionally.

Provide them multiple environments to interface with so that they can broaden their own worldview. While on an outing listen to their voices to discover what they are saying and most importantly what they are not saying. Never judge their life, communities, relationships, or identities. Other things to consider while mentoring Males of Color:

- You should function in the role of student to gain an intimate understanding of the struggles in which these young men experience.
- Value their lived experiences.
- Allow your engagement to be fluid and do not force your values, beliefs, and ideologies upon them.
- Make sure your actions are in line with your statements by being a living epistle and role model.
- Do not view Black and Latino males as monolithic beings but as individuals who bring multiple perspectives to the worlds they inhabit.

A Quick Message for Black and Latino Males
And Those Who Love, Love, Work and Educate Them!

Not all Black and Latino men in America are committed to a life of criminality. Many of us are committed to our professions, families, and our communities. I believe for every negative image of us spewed across the television and the Internet, there are many more positive images of who we are and the lives we live. The challenges of our communities are rooted in our own self-image. Everything we see about our image in popular culture is digitally enhanced and (re) packaged for consumption. The economic gain does not benefit our communities or our self-worth. We must also not be complicit in this production. The responsibility is ours and ours alone. We must be vigilant in the quest to transform our own lives if we want our lineage to continue. As a black male, I implore you to understand that I know you are human beings and you desire the same things everyone else does--love, security, financial independence and the opportunity to be affirmed. You must take your life back from the hands of defeat. You must decide your own fate and believe your destiny resides in both the hands of your CREATOR and yours as well. It is never too late to change and seek out ways and resources to become better. You are the captain of your ship and only you can take the helm of your destiny and steer the rudder and sails into the winds of SUCCESS! I salute you and your efforts. Keep praying; hold on to your faith and continue to do DOING WHAT IS RIGHT!

A Quick Message for Higher Education

Educators, who come to the academy in which I serve, are searching for answers. These individuals struggle with how to implement local, state and federal legislation, seek efficient and effective ways to provide optimal learning experiences for all members of the learning community and strive to make sense of the dynamic cultures in which they work professionally. During this era of market competition, globalization and educational accountability the challenge of the academy is transforming those aspiring educational leaders who are concerned more with "the bottom line," into critically consciousness democratic leaders who seek to develop free thinking members of our society. Given the call for "principal executives," democratic education and freedom have been reduced to the ability to achieve academic standards and acquire material goods, wealth, and power without critiquing the consequences of inequity, greed, and inequality.

The national economic downturn, the last wave of horrific budget cuts, the present political climate are adding to the hurdles for educators, particularly administrators, who must successfully educate students with less than adequate resources. These resources are not just monetary but human as well. The current socio-cultural political climate in the United States, the renewing of the Patriot Act, disaster relief or the lack thereof, terrorism and homeland security, the demonization of those in poverty, and the privatization of free public education forces me to ask the following central question: What is the promise and purpose of a democratic education? Higher education and K-12 public schooling has changed significantly within the past ten years. The advancement of the democratic promise of public education continues to be challenged by political and economic forces, which constrain the opportunities for America's citizenry to enhance the value of one's life by accessing public colleges and universities and by benefiting from a "free" public education. The work in which we do must engaged the communities in which we inhabit not as subjects to be researched, but as collaborators in the process of inquiry, if we seek to transform our humanity. Public schools are the basic foundation for developing an informed citizenry, fully capable of self-governance. They are capable not because of the tools we provide, but because they arrive to school with a critical consciousness that allows them to question. It is up to us to enhance the skills of those we teach so they will be able to awaken that consciousness.

Given the promise of public education, I ask each of you to focus on the following questions:

- What are the pedagogical challenges of co-creating democratic spaces with practitioners to provide for seamless learning through the K-20 educational experience?
- How do we collaborate, (re) create, and (re) conceptualize institutions and systems of education into affirming, dynamic, and engaging learning communities that are anti-oppressive and inclusive?

As a creative educational leader who embodies education as praxis of freedom my perspective of democracy is evidenced in my practice. I strive to co-create learning environments where all member-voices are given the opportunity to be heard, shared and awakened. The dialogic encounter is central to (de) constructing and (re) constructing spaces for knowledge acquisition and development. In order for the citizens of the United States to continue to engage in "life, liberty and the pursuit of happiness," democracy must exist in institutions that encourage human beings to transform our environment, communities, neighborhoods, and schools into arenas where dialogue, discourse, and dissent are not silenced but celebrated. The aforementioned should be the foci of K-20 public and private education in the United States. Instead of continuing to view public schools as sites of reform we must transform the role, function and purpose of schooling. Those of us who teach in Colleges of Education realize the importance of language and how it informs practice. Moving students from the language of reformation to transformation is often difficult and viewed as counter-productive; however if schools are to be sites of democracy this is the path of liberation. I encourage students to view themselves not as mere custodians of buildings of learning, but as proactive transformational leaders. Such a role involves understanding the schools culture and transforming custodial organizations into creative learning communities. This change requires transformational leadership that is creative, courageous, and visionary.

Finally

As an African American male academician many of the critical perspectives regarding the intersections of race, class, and gender affront the white Southern Christian values many of my students' hold near and dear. The expectation is for me to operate out of false civility and behave as if these values should not be critiqued and/or interrogated, but honored and celebrated regardless of how they assault the plurality of values students bring into public schools daily. Coupled this with my being a faculty of member of color, regardless of credentials, ideological orientation and instructional style my students at times implicitly and explicitly challenge my professorial authority, scholarship, intellect, and political agenda. After speaking truth to power in many of our dialogic encounters I have often heard students call me "the angry black man" or "Dr. Thug." I find it interesting how they construct my passion for the subject and fiery delivery style as a place of subjugation. Given the atrocities occurring in public education in our nation today we should all be angered to action.

In order to transform schools we must hold our students accountable. We do this by shifting them from a traditionalist view of education and democracy to one that is radical and transformative. We can do this by promoting environments which require students to engage in independent thinking, motivate them to take ownership of their learning process, and by providing opportunities for rigorous intellectual study and committed activism that moves beyond arriving at the "right" answers. This requires critical change in teaching Prek-20.

Teaching is political as well as a liberatory practice. Our nation's freedom depends upon the development of enticing and exciting democratic learning communities where the pursuit of knowledge is the primary objective. Because American democracy is under a re-construction situated within globalization, evangelical fundamentalism, free market enterprise and socio-cultural politics the educational leader of today must be able to negotiate and navigate the often competing and conflicting forces of our democracy. Teaching, learning and leading democratically require constant participation with change. The purpose of higher education and K-12 public education is to provide opportunities and spaces for the global citizenry to engage in democratic practices for the public good. Democracy is an enacted daily practice whereby people interact and relate through daily personal, social, and professional routines with a primary focus on continuing the betterment of our humanity. This is the cause of education. In order to do this higher education must prepare critical transformative leaders who are willing and able to draw upon culturally relevant, critical, and counter-normative pedagogies. I do this by infusing cultural studies in the leadership discourse of our educational leadership program.

Critical change occurs with significant self-sacrifice, potential alienation, rejection and costly consequences. As critical transformative educators, we must do justice to the larger social/public responsibility of our positions and roles, particularly in higher education. In (re) crafting the education of critical transformative leaders, we must demystify change, courage, and risk as we (re) imagine the language and fluency of multiple discourses in the rediscovery of democracy and social justice. This occurs in the development of the democratic classroom, which should be the hallmark of higher education.

Critical transformative educational leaders who develop through the seamless K-20 educational system in the United States will facilitate the development of inviting, engaging and dynamic learning communities that (1) transform the human condition, (2) unearth fallow ground, (3) interrogate and rupture the status quo, (4) question multiple political spaces critically, (5) seek multiple epistemologies to re-create constructs that better serve our humanity. To further our thinking regarding the challenges of seamless learning from K-20, I call on all higher education faculty members who actively serve in teacher education and/or educational leadership preparation programs around the country to (re) think the following:

We are educating in a time of expanding globalization whose impact we witness via 24-hour digitally mediated discourse. How are schools and educational leaders keeping up with this global transformation? What type of impact does this transformation of schools from sites of democracy to "bedfellows" of consumerism have upon the school and much larger global community? How are the "souls" of schools affected? In the journey of school reform are educational leaders acknowledging that the "process of schooling" is filled with "cultural politics"? How are educational leadership programs preparing future school leaders? Are educational leadership preparation programs equipping schools' leaders for the "journey of the self" or for the "journey of the soul"?

As a critical transformative educational leader I inspire and transform others to become more conscious of the human condition. My teaching and practice is oriented toward social vision and change, not simply, or only, organizational goals. My teaching is a form of protest and activism. Because I view my self as a teacher-activist, I understand that it is my duty and responsibility to encourage other human beings, particularly those who are involved in the educational process, to transform our environment, institutions, communities, neighborhoods, and schools into arenas where those in which we come in contact will become agents of democracy and social justice. Together we must face the struggle of educating our citizenry with nobility and commitment. For together in the struggle we are one.

Websites/Resources

The Superintendent's Desk
www.thesuperintendentsdesk.com

Forum, Resources, and Links for practicing & aspiring Superintendents

The Principal's Desk
www.theprincipalsdesk.com

Forum, Resources, and Links for practicing & aspiring Principals

The Vice-Principal's Desk
www.theviceprincipalsdesk.com

Forum, Resources, and Links for practicing & aspiring Vice-Principals

Black Masculinity
www.blackmasculinity.com

A site designed to "critique," "question," and "de-center" Black Masculinity

Black Male PhD
www.blackmalephd.com

Forum, Resources, Links, and Support for "Brothers" with terminal degrees and for those who aspire to achieve their terminal degree

GLBTIQQ
www.glbtiqq.com

Forum, Resources, Educational Materials, and support for those who self-identify within the following continuum: Gay, Lesbian, Bi-sexual Transgendered, Intersex, Queer, and Questioning. This site is also designed for allies, educators, those individuals who love GLBTIQQ peoples, as well as a place to investigate, interrogate, and question the heteronormative.

ABD Not Me!
www.abdnotme.com

This site is for all of those individuals who are currently completing terminal degrees, those who completed course-work but nothing else, those who are having difficulty beginning and/or completing the dissertation process, and those who are feeling lost within the process. After experiencing many of the students whose committees I chair have "emotional" and "mental" breakdowns all within the same week and hearing each of them say to me in some way, "I must be stupid, I know I am the only one going through this and I feel so alone and disconnected," I realized an online support community would be great for them and others.

UNCG-OEDI
www.uncgoedi.com

Forum, Resources, Links and Initiative-generator for UNC-Greensboro, Office of Equity, Diversity, and Inclusion. This site is not an official site of UNCG and it is not sanctioned by UNC-Greensboro.

Additional Works by C. P. Gause, PhD

Books

Gause, C. P. (2008). *Integration matters: navigating identity, culture and resistance.* New York: Peter Lang. *2009 American Education Studies Association Critics' Choice Award*

Carlson, D. & Gause, C. P. (2007). (Ed.). *Keeping the promise: Essays on leadership, democracy and education.* New York: Peter Lang. *2007 American Education Studies Association Critics' Choice Award*

Published Articles/Book Chapters (Peer-Reviewed)

Gause, C. P. & **Okun, T**. (In-Press). What's Love Got To Do With It: Sexuality, Education, and Capitalism. In D. Carlson & D. Roseboro (Eds.). The Sexuality Curriculum: Youth Culture, Popular Culture, and Progressive Sexuality Education. (Book Chapter)

Poole, J. & Gause, C. P. (In-Press). Under Construction: Rural Spaces and Sexual Identities. In T. Quinn & E. R. Meiners (Eds.). Sexualities in Education: A Reader. (Book Chapter)

Gause, C. P., Perrin, D., & Dennison, S. (In-Press). Equity, Inclusiveness, and Diversifying the Faculty: Transforming the University in the 21st Century. *Quest* (Journal)

*Bold connotes collaboration with current and/or former doctoral students.

Douglas, T. & Gause, C. P. (In-Press). Beacons of Light in Oceans of Darkness: Exploring Black Bermudian Masculinity. *Learning for Democracy*. (Journal)

Gause, C. P. (In-press). Veiling the Queer. In D. Chapman (Eds.). *Teaching Social Theory: Crossing Borders and Reflecting Back*. Peter Lang: New York. (Book Chapter)

Gause, C. P., **Okun, T., Stalnaker, A., Nix-Stevenson, D., Chapman, D.**, (2009). The Counterstory and the promise of collaborative compassion in education. *Learning for Democracy*, 3 (1). (Journal)

Gause, C. P. (2008). From social justice to collaborative activism: changing the landscape of academic leadership. *Academic Leadership: The Online Journal*, 6(3). http://www.academicleadership.org/emprical_research/From_So cial_Justice_to_Collaborative_Activism_Changing_the_Landscape _of_Academic_Leadership.shtml (Journal)

Roseboro, D. & Gause, C. P. (2009). Faculty of color constructing communities at predominantly White institutions. In C. A. Mullen (Ed.), *Leadership and building professional learning communities*. New York: Palgrave Macmillan. (Book Chapter)

Gause, C. P. (2009). Uncovering truth: In search of a "BMSALA" (Black Male Same-Affection-Loving Academician). In S. R. Steinberg (Ed.), *Diversity and multiculturalism: A Reader*. New York: Peter Lang. (Book Chapter)

*Bold connotes collaboration with current and/or former doctoral students.

Gause, C. P. (2008). Old school meets new school: unsettling times at freedom junior-senior high. *Journal of Cases in Educational Leadership*. 10.1177/1555458908314504v1.pdf http://jel.sagepub.com hosted at http://online.sagepub.com (Journal)

Gause, C. P., Reitzug, U. R., & Villaverde, L. (2007). Beyond generic democracy: Holding our students accountable for democratic leadership and practice. In D. Carlson & C. P. Gause (Eds.), *Keeping the promise: Essays on leadership, democracy and education* (pp. 217-231). New York: Peter Lang. (Book Chapter)

Cooper, C. W., & Gause, C.P. (2007). Who's afraid of the big bad wolf? Facing identity politics and resistance when teaching for social justice. In D. Carlson & C. P. Gause (Eds.), *Keeping the promise: Essays on leadership, democracy and education* (pp. 197-216). New York: Peter Lang. (Book Chapter)

Gause, C. P., **Okun, T., Chapman, D., Nix-Stevenson, D., Stalnaker, A**. (2007). The Counterstory and the promise of collaborative compassion in education. In David C. Thompson and Faith E. Crampton (Eds.), Fostering compassion and understanding across borders: An international dialogue on the future of educational leadership. UCEA Conference Proceedings for convention 2007. http://coe.ksu.edu/ucea/byauthor.htm (Journal)

Gause, C. P. (2007). Beyond the politics of K-20 education: navigating, negotiating, and transgressing the academy—a brother speaks! *Thresholds in Education Journal, XXXIII* (4), 8-13. (Journal)

*Bold connotes collaboration with current and/or former doctoral students.

Capper, C., Alston, J., Gause, C.P., Korsoreck, J. Lopez, G., Lugg C., McKenzie, K. (2006). Integrating gay/lesbian/bisexual/transgender topics and their intersections with other areas of difference into the leadership preparation curriculum: practical ideas and strategies. Special Issue *Journal of School Leadership, 16*(2), 142-157. (Journal)

Gause, C. P. (2005). The ghetto sophisticates: performing black masculinity, saving lost souls and serving as leaders of the new school. *Taboo: The Journal of Culture and Education, 9*(1), 17-31. (Journal)

Gause, C. P. (2005). Guest Editor Theme Issue "Edu-Tainment": Introduction-popular culture in the making of schools for the 21st century. *Journal of School Leadership, 15*(3), 240-242. (Journal)

Gause, C. P. (2005). Navigating the stormy seas: critical perspectives on the intersection of popular culture and educational leader-"Ship." *Journal of School Leadership, 15*(3), 333-342. (Journal)

Gause, C. P. (2003). Transforming leaders, creating communities: changing schools through transformative leadership, Commentary-Miami University, Department of Educational Leadership-Electronic Journal: *Initiative Anthology.* http://www.units.muohio.edu/eap/departments/edl/eduleadership/anthology/RCI/COM03002.html. (Journal).

*Bold connotes collaboration with current and/or former doctoral students.

Gause, C. P. (2002). What you see is not always what you get. The role of popular culture in today's middle school. *South Carolina Middle School Journal, 10*(1) 26-29. (Journal)

C. Published Articles/Creative Works (Non-Peer Reviewed)

Gause, C. P. (2008). Today: I opened my eyes. In *Integration Matters: Navigating Identity, Culture and Resistance.* New York: Peter Lang. 157-159

Gause, C.P. (2008). Brother denied. In *Integration Matters: Navigating Identity, Culture and Resistance.* New York: Peter Lang. 61-62

Gause, C.P. (2008). Not I but we. In UNCG-Educational Leadership and Cultural Foundations, Department Newsletter, *Organic Unity*, Vol. 1 (1). Pg. 7 http://www.uncg.edu/elc/ELC%20Newsletter/ELC_Newsletter _Organic_Unity_Vol1_Iss1.pdf

Gause, C. P. (2006). Man of fire—man of passion *Chicken Bones: A Journal for Literary & Artistic African-American Themes.* http://www.nathanielturner.com/manoffiremanofpassioncpgause .htm

Gause, C.P. (2005/2001). Bitter. In The Ghetto Sophisticates: Performing Black Masculinity, Saving Lost Souls and Serving as Leaders of the New School. *Taboo: The Journal of Culture and Education,* 9 (1), 17-31.

D. Book Reviews

Gause, C. (2003). Review of *Performing Identity/ Performing Text*, by Greg Dimitriadis. *Urban Education, 38* (1) January 2003.

About the Author

Dr. C. P. Gause is an Associate Professor in the Department of Educational Leadership and Cultural Foundations at The University of North Carolina at Greensboro. He is also Co-chair of the Chancellor's Advisory Committee on Equity, Diversity and Inclusion. A former public school teacher, principal, and K-12 school administrator Gause received his Ph.D. in Educational Leadership from Miami University. He is co-editor of *Keeping the Promise: Essays on Leadership, Democracy and Education* (Peter Lang, 2007), a recipient of the 2007 American Educational Studies Association Critics Choice Award. His research interests include gender and queer studies; black masculinity; cultural studies; critical race theory; critical spirituality; and collaborative activism. He is author of *Integration Matters: Navigating, Identity, Culture and Resistance* (Peter Lang, 2008) a recipient of the 2009 American Educational Studies Association Critics Choice Award. This groundbreaking volume constructs a blueprint for realizing academic achievement and academic success for all students, particularly those who are members of under-represented populations.

Contact Information:
C. P. Gause, PhD
GES-Gause Educational Solutions, LLC
2523 Wheatfield Drive
Greensboro, NC 27405

Email: drcpgause@gmail.com
Website: www.drcpgause.com